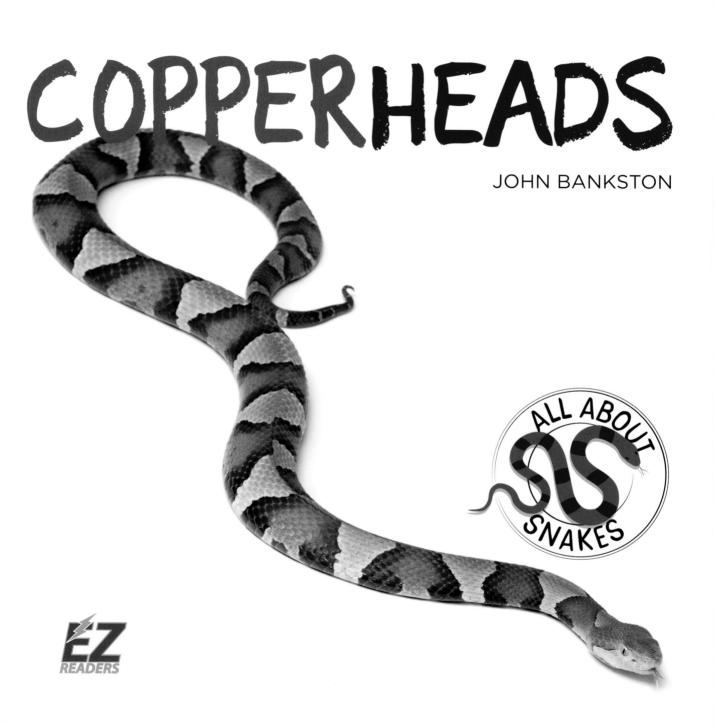

COPPERHEADS

JOHN BANKSTON

ALL ABOUT SNAKES

EZ READERS

Creating Young Nonfiction Readers

EZ Readers lets children delve into nonfiction at beginning reading levels. Young readers are introduced to new concepts, facts, ideas, and vocabulary.

Tips for Reading Nonfiction with Beginning Readers

Talk about Nonfiction
Begin by explaining that nonfiction books give us information that is true. The book will be organized around a specific topic or idea, and we may learn new facts through reading.

Look at the Parts
Most nonfiction books have helpful features. Our *EZ Readers* include a Contents page, an index, a picture glossary, and color photographs. Share the purpose of these features with your reader.

Contents
Located at the front of a book, the Contents displays a list of the big ideas within the book and where to find them.

Index
An index is an alphabetical list of topics and the page numbers where they are found.

Picture Glossary
Located at the back of the book, a picture glossary contains key words/phrases that are related to the topic.

Photos/Charts
A lot of information can be found by "reading" the charts and photos found within nonfiction text. Help your reader learn more about the different ways information can be displayed.

With a little help and guidance about reading nonfiction, you can feel good about introducing a young reader to the world of *EZ Readers* nonfiction books.

Mitchell Lane
PUBLISHERS

2001 SW 31st Avenue
Hallandale, FL 33009
www.mitchelllane.com

First Edition, 2019.

Author: John Bankston
Designer: Ed Morgan
Editor: Sharon F. Doorasamy

Names/credits:
Title: Copperheads / by John Bankston
Description: Hallandale, FL : Mitchell Lane Publishers, [2019]

Series: All About Snakes

Library bound ISBN: 9781680203097

eBook ISBN: 9781680203103

EZ readers is an imprint of Mitchell Lane Publishers

Photo credits: Getty Images, Freepik.com, public domain

CONTENTS

Copperhead snakes hide in places like piles of leaves. They aren't very big. They are as long as your arm.

Copperheads live in the woods. They swim. They climb. They blend. They look like their **environment**.

Copperheads range across the eastern United States. They make their homes from Florida to Massachusetts.

Copperheads come in shades of red. Their heads are copper red. Their bodies are reddish brown. Brown **bands** circle their skin.

11

They are pit vipers. They have pits on their head. Copperheads feel heat. This helps them find prey.

Copperheads eat mice. They also enjoy lizards, bugs, and other snakes.

They bite without warning.

Copperheads are venomous snakes. Their bite can make you sick.

Copperheads share a den in the winter. Scared copperheads pretend to freeze instead of escaping. They smell like cucumbers.

INTERESTING FACTS

- Copperheads don't lay eggs. They give birth to little snakes. Baby snakes are also **venomous**.

- Female copperheads are usually longer than males.

- They can live 18 years.

- In the spring and fall, copperheads are awake during the day. In the summer, they stay up all night.

PARTS OF A COPPERHEAD

Head
Copperheads have pits between their eyes and the **nostrils** on both sides of the head. This lets them tell when warm prey is nearby. The longer the snake, the longer its fangs.

Body
Snakes have a spine or backbone made up of many vertebrae attached to ribs. Copperheads have more than 100 **vertebrae**. People have 33. A snake's vertebrae expand when it eats.

Tail
The thinner part of the snake where there are no ribs. Although females are longer, males have a longer tail.

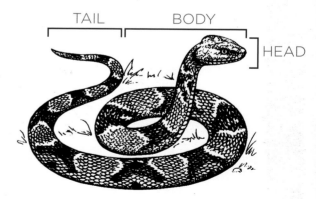

TAIL BODY HEAD

GLOSSARY

bands
A stripe or strip of color

cucumbers
Long, green-skinned fruit

environment
Nature; the air, water,
and land that animals live in or on

nostril
A part of the nose

prey
An animal that is hunted by another animal

range
Area where an animal lives

venomous
Poisonous

vertebrae
Small bones that make up the backbone

FURTHER READING

Books

Bell, Samantha. *Copperheads*. Minneapolis, MN: Core Library, an imprint of ABDO Publishing, 2015.

Dunn, Mary R. *Copperheads*. North Mankato, MN: Capstone Press, 2014.

Gunderson, Megan M. *Copperheads*. Edina, MN: ABDO, 2010.

Howard, Melanie A. *Copperheads*. Mankato, MN: Capstone Press, 2012.

On the Internet

https://www.livescience.com/43641-copperhead-snake.html

http://animals.mom.me/interesting-copperheads-9300.html

https://nationalzoo.si.edu/animals/northern-copperhead

WORKS CONSULTED

"Copperheads." *Highlights for Children*, September 2014.

"What's the difference between poisonous and venomous animals?" *Ranger Rick*, May 1997.

Amistaadt, Axl J. "Interesting Facts About Copperheads." http://animals.mom.me/interesting-copperheads-9300.html.

Andrews, Kimberly, and Willson, J. D. "Copperhead (Agkistrodon contortrix) - Venomous." Savannah River Ecology Laboratory, University of Georgia. https://srelherp.uga.edu/snakes/agkcon.htm.

"Northern Copperhead." Smithsonian National Zoo and Conservation Biology Institute. https://nationalzoo.si.edu/animals/northern-copperhead.

Szalay, Jessie. "Copperhead Snakes: Facts, Bites & Babies," *Live Science*, November 19, 2014. https://www.livescience.com/43641-copperhead-snake.html.

INDEX